The Professional Woman's Guide to Managing Men

Gain confidence and earn respect with this step-by-step guide for female leaders

Anna Runyan

The Professional Woman's Guide to Managing Men

First published: November 2013

Production Reference: 2211113

Published by Impackt Publishing Ltd.
Livery Place
35 Livery Street
Birmingham B3 2PB, UK.

ISBN 978-1-78300-028-9

www.Impacktpub.com

Cover Image by Jarek Blaminsky (milak6@wp.pl)

Credits

Author

Anna Runyan

Reviewers

Lisa A. Fredin

Melynda Harbour

Commissioning Editors

Stephanie Moss

Danielle Rosen

Copy Editors

Jalasha D'costa

Maria Gould

Paul Hindle

Project Coordinators

Priyanka Goel

Anurag Banerjee

Proofreaders

Maria Gould

Paul Hindle

Simran Bhogal

Ameesha Green

Indexer

Hemangini Bari

Production Coordinator

Melwyn D'sa

Cover Work

Melwyn D'sa

Foreword

The other day I found myself listening to an interview with Sheryl Sandberg regarding her book, Lean In.

She said as recently as two years ago, that often-asked question of "what it's like to be a woman leader" made her bristle.

And so she gave the standard answer.

You know the one.

"I'm not a woman leader. I'm a leader."

Fortunately for us, Sheryl has changed her tune and, in the process, cracked open the door to—finally—have some dialogue about gender differences at work.

Because the truth is what you're about to read has been needed for a long time.

Seriously. As much as everyone loves to neuter the workforce, women and men AREN'T the same.

And thank God.

History (and countless studies) prove that diverse teams make better decisions, but the fact that women have had to work so hard to get a seat at the table has made gender at work a particularly touchy subject.

So there it was.

Thorny.

Debated in periphery.

And yet never fully addressed.

There's no question we have all reaped the benefits of three waves of pioneering sheroes, but while it's always important to remember the past, it's also important to look to the future.

In other words, now that we've made it this far, how do we embody our full potential?

So, let's get honest.

If you want to lead big, you have to know how to lead men – and that ain't easy.

Good thing you found this book.

Because in these pages you will learn how to earn respect by focusing on what matters, leveraging your strengths, and being professional without being a robot in heels.

You also have the benefit of a guide as sharp as Anna.

Indeed, as we watch the number of women leaders slowly but steadily rise and stand on remarkable platforms of accomplishment in business, we owe a collective hat tip to women like her and books like this.

I hope you soak in every page.

To your success –

Emily Bennington
Founder of Awake Exec™ Conscious Career Design
Author of Who Says It's a Man's World: The Girls' Guide to Corporate Domination

About the Author

Anna Runyan has successfully worked in a male-dominated field for seven years as a Government Consultant at Booz Allen Hamilton. She is a Career Coach and Founder of one of the top career development blogs, ClassyCareerGirl.com, which recently made the Forbes "Top 100 Websites For Your Career" list. She is also Professor of Career Development and Management at DeVry University and her career advice has been featured in Forbes, Yahoo! Finance, and People StyleWatch magazine. Anna lives with her husband, John, in San Diego.

Get more career advice and inspiration from Anna Runyan at ClassyCareerGirl.com.

Acknowledgments

After writing a blog daily for almost four years, I thought writing a book would be a piece of cake. Boy, was I wrong. This is my very first book (of many I hope) and I can tell you that it changed me. It was so much harder than I ever would have thought and I grew so much from writing it. I would not have gotten through this journey of writing my first book without the help and support from many people.

Thanks to everyone at Impackt Publishing who made this book possible and the very best it could be.

To my biggest fans—my parents, Sue Burger and Ron Burger, and mother-in-law, Jan Runyan. Thank you for reading every word I say and being so supportive of everything I do.

To my husband, John, for being my behind-the-scenes coach. You are truly the secret to my success and I couldn't imagine doing this journey of life without you.

Thank you to my assistant, Lor, who helps me get everything I need to get done... somehow.

Thank you to Emily Bennington for inspiring me and writing the foreword to this book. I won't forget to pay it forward.

Thank you to Lisa Fredin and Melynda Harbour who reviewed every word I wrote and made this book even better. You ladies rock!

To my very first coaching client, Erin Sheedy. You got me started!

And, thank you to everyone who has ever read my blog. I hope that I have inspired you and thank you so much for sharing this journey with me. Without readers, I wouldn't be able to write so thank you for reading and pushing me to write this book.

About the Reviewer

Lisa A. Fredin has a Ph.D in Materials and Theoretical Chemistry and has spent her career in multiple large collaborative work groups at a variety of cutting edge research universities, including working abroad in Sweden. In a field that is often still male-dominated, especially at the highest levels of academia, the vast majority of colleges, supervisors, and subordinates in Lisa's career have been male. She recognizes that mentoring and managing new scientists is a critical skill for any supervisor and learning to do this well for both men and women is crucial not just for her own career but to increase the representation of women at the top of any field.

Dedicated to my parents, Sue and Ron, who taught me to dream big and that I could be anything I ever wanted to be.

Contents

> Preface

Managing the "Boys' Club"

Recently, I was speaking about this book to a middle-aged man in the military. He asked me:

> *"What makes you qualified to write a book about managing men?"*

If you have ever had a man question your knowledge and expertise, you know that it can make you feel like you aren't good enough. When this man questioned me that day, I could have lost my confidence and gotten angry with him. I could have started to question why I was even writing this book and just stopped writing altogether.

But, this was not the first time I felt like a man questioned my knowledge and expertise. Little did he know that what I was writing my book about was exactly how to handle his question confidently. I told him the following:

> *"I have spent the past seven years working with and managing men as a consultant to the U.S. Navy. I have managed men who were shocked to have a woman in charge, which wasn't always easy. It took me a while to figure out how best to work with and manage men. There were many times that I had no idea what to do and I tried many different things to see what worked. I treated men I managed in the same way I thought a man would treat them. That didn't work. Then, I treated them how I treated other women. That didn't work either. It wasn't until I started to just be myself and lean on my own female leadership strengths that I began to successfully start gaining trust and respect from the men I managed."*

I gained respect that day from this man because I was confident in my book's topic and myself. I want to help you gain this same confidence so you can build trust and respect with the men you manage today and in the future.

You are not alone

If you are about to start managing men or have managed men in the past and want to have more success, you may be nervous about where to start. You might be worried about coming across as too strong, aggressive, or bitchy. You might not be confident in yourself because you don't really understand men. You might be uncomfortable, awkward, and quiet around the men you work with. I was. I could relate more with women on my team but I knew that understanding men was the key to getting promoted and having more leadership opportunities. Learning how to manage both genders successfully was the key for me to finally getting ahead at work.

In 2010, I created a career development blog geared specifically toward professional women called ClassyCareerGirl.com. I receive questions daily about how to manage and work with men. Here are some of the e-mails I have received:

"My boss is a male and I lead a team of men. I am 9 months into this position and I am really trying to get a handle on leading men."

"I have always worked with men, it has always been a challenge for me to manage the "boys' club." Working with men is a big challenge, not only having to gain their trust but also to discover what motivates them mentally. It's a task trying to become "one of the boys."

"Most of my male co-workers are older and I find it tough to interact with them in a work setting without feeling awkward. I am scared they will think of me like their daughter or unintentionally flirtatious."

"I will soon be managing 10 employees over 70 percent male. This prospect has to be the largest source of doubt on my ability to achieve my current goals."

"I would like to learn more about what it is like to manage men. How I can stay strong and confident and not let them intimidate me in the workplace? I need your expertise to know what to expect!"

"I want to prove that in the work field, it is not our sex that makes the difference, but what we know and can do."

And then I got another e-mail from a woman who has figured out the secret like I have:

"Now as a top agent in my market, I work with men daily on the big deals. Knowing how to "speak their language" is crucial to my success."

In this book, I will teach you how to speak their language and how to learn what motivates men. After you read this book, you will no longer be intimidated at work.

My mission

As a Career Coach, I focus exclusively on helping women get their careers unstuck, helping them find work they love and get ahead. When you build the trust and respect with the men on your team, you gain all three of these things I teach. You will be happier at work (sometimes their jokes are funny!), you will gain confidence to go for that management or executive position, and you will zoom in on your female strengths, making you even more successful at work. My goal is to help women who were once nervous about managing and working with men to become confident in what they bring to the table. No longer will you feel like you have to be unlike yourself to fit in, because you will know your unique managerial style and know what goes on inside a man's head. There are many stereotypes and double standards that women often have to break at work. My goal is that this book will help you brush those stereotypes aside, be confident in your strengths, and be the best leader that you can possibly be. Whether you are already in a career managing men or preparing yourself for a career working with men, this book is for you.

The facts about women at work

The statistics show that women make a great addition to work teams. Pepperdine researchers found Fortune 500 firms with the best record of promoting women to senior positions are 69 percent more profitable than the median Fortune 500 companies in their industries. Our time is now, and more opportunities are available for women in the workplace than ever before.

But, the rate of turnover in management positions is 2.5 times higher among top-performing women than it is among men. In addition, females held only 14 percent of executive officer positions at Fortune 500 companies in 2012. One of my hypotheses for these statistics is that women are not managing their business relationships with men as effectively as they could. From my experience, women are good at building great relationships with other women they work with but not with the men they work with. Women are not getting into the tight networks that the men are making where opportunities and connections are made in the "boys' network."

 The bad news is that women are not getting into the conversations with men they need to be getting into. My book teaches you how to get into that "boys' club", and how to develop that trust and build those relationships so that we can increase the percentage of women in top leadership positions.

What this book covers

Chapter 1, Focus on You First, will teach you how to use the strengths that you have right now, to be the best manager possible at work tomorrow. We will cover how to focus on your female strengths, how to stop being a perfectionist, and how to find your unique leadership style.

Chapter 2, How to be a Confident Female Manager, will teach you why it is important to be self-confident when managing men and how to own the room when you walk into it. We will cover how to be assertive, how to communicate with men, and how you can promote yourself without being obnoxious.

Chapter 3, How to Help the Men on Your Team Thrive, will teach you how to use men's love for competition and gamesmanship for the success of your team. We'll cover how to embrace men's love for competition, how to use humor to lighten things up, how to do office sports talk, how to build trust with the men you manage, and how to coach the men on your team.

Chapter 4, What NOT to do When Managing Men, will teach you common mistakes female managers make when managing men. We'll cover how to not get too personal at work with men, how to not play the role of "office mom", and how to draw the line with office relationships.

Chapter 5, Handling Common Management Situations, will teach you how to handle common management situations that you will most likely encounter while managing men. We'll cover how to provide feedback to men, how to handle social events with men, and how to negotiate with men.

How to use this book

"Success is the sum of small efforts, repeated day in and day out."

—Robert Collier

This isn't just a regular book that you read and put back on your shelf. This entire book was written as a "how-to" guidebook with specific action steps you can take while reading. If you aren't going to take action with what you learn, read no further. I want you to commit to yourself; take notes, answer the questions at the end of each chapter, and really try to become a better manager as you read through this book.

If you are currently a manager, I recommend reading one chapter a week and actually putting what you learn into practice each week at work. If you are not yet a manager, I recommend keeping a journal of what you are learning so that you can reference it once you get that manager position someday. I also want you to start acting like a manager even if you aren't yet one because that is the quickest way you will become a manager. Even if you aren't a manager yet, I want you to start using the principles you learn in this book to improve your relationships with all men that you work with right now. (You can even practice them with your personal relationships with men if you like, but improved marriages and sibling relationships are not guaranteed).

Pretend that I am your own personal coach cheering you on as you walk into your next meeting. I am behind you every step of the way!

P.S. Please stop by, say hello, and receive additional career inspiration at www.classycareergirl.com.

Conventions

In this book, you will find a number of styles of text that distinguish between different kinds of information. Here are some examples of these styles, and an explanation of their meaning.

New terms and **important words** are shown in bold.

 Warnings or important notes appear in a box like this.

 Tips and tricks appear like this.

 Activities or exercises to be performed appear like this.

Reader feedback

Feedback from our readers is always welcome. Let us know what you think about this book—what you liked or may have disliked, or even if you have any questions. Reader feedback is important for us to develop titles that you really get the most out of.

To send us general feedback, simply send an e-mail to contact@impacktpublishing.com and mention the book title in the subject of your message.

If there is a topic that you have expertise in and you are interested in either writing or contributing to a book, you can also use the link or e-mail address above. One of our editors will get back to you within a week to discuss your idea further.

Piracy

Piracy of copyright material on the Internet is an ongoing problem across all media. At Impackt, we take the protection of our copyright and licenses very seriously. If you come across any illegal copies of our works—in any form—on the Internet, please provide us with the location address or website name immediately so that we can pursue a remedy.

Please contact us at copyright@impacktpublishing.com with a link to the suspected pirated material.

We appreciate your help in protecting our authors, and our ability to bring you valuable content.

>1

Focus on You First

In this chapter, you will learn how to use the strengths that you have right now to be the best manager possible at work tomorrow. After you have read this chapter, you will be more comfortable leading the men on your team.

We will cover:

- ➤ How to focus on your female strengths
- ➤ How to stop being a perfectionist
- ➤ How to find your unique leadership style

Focusing on your female strengths

A common concern many new female managers have is their lack of management experience, especially experience managing the opposite sex. What many women don't realize is that they already have certain natural qualities that are going to make them great managers, just as men naturally develop leadership strengths such as risk taking and seeking out new competitive opportunities at a young age.

For example, in my senior year of college, I had a part-time job, an internship, a full-time class schedule, and a boyfriend. That year, not only did I learn how to multitask and manage my own time, but I also learned how to stay calm and graceful during tough situations such as living with five girls in a two-bedroom apartment. I never would have thought that year of busy chaos was preparing me to be a great manager someday. The skills I acquired helped me to step into a management situation where not only did I need to manage my own tasks, but I also needed to manage the tasks of other people.

I can go back even further to see myself developing the skills I use most today as a manager—skills such as coaching and mentoring. I was always the go-to-gal through high school. I was the one my friends would seek out for advice on anything from ditching their boyfriends to getting into college. Mentoring and coaching are natural strengths that I now apply as a woman who manages men.

I have learned to focus on the strengths I know I have to quickly develop trust with the men I manage. When managing women, I don't have to focus as much on my strengths because it is more natural for me to speak to and manage a woman due to our similar strengths. The table in the following section will help you identify what strengths you have right now that you can use from day one as a new manager of men.

Common female leadership strengths

In my experience, there are many qualities that female managers inherently have that men appreciate. Men often have different strengths than women, and that is why diverse teams of men and women work well together. Review the following table of strengths and think about what strong points you already have.

It's also important to know that many of these leadership strengths can also be disadvantages if taken too far. While many of the following strengths are good qualities, at times they can be double-edged swords. Women have to balance their traits so that they can gain the trust and respect of men. They need to learn how to "play" to their audience, which is why I have also included ways that these strengths can be a disadvantage if taken too far.

Attribute	Description
Collaboration	Women often request ideas from the entire team and get group buy-in. Women are also great at sharing information and delegating.
	How will this help you?
	Men want to belong to a team and be empowered to make decisions and participate. Men appreciate that not everything is based on competition with a woman.
	When this strength can be a disadvantage
	When a female manager cannot make a decision without getting team collaboration. Men want their managers to be decisive.
Calm under pressure	Women can handle tough situations with a sense of calm and without getting aggressive. Women can also appear less threatening by establishing trust quickly with the men they manage.
	How will this help you?
	Men are often not emotional at work. During tough situations, men want a manager that can resolve conflicts quickly without creating anxiety and chaos. Men also want to have a non-threatening manager so they can feel comfortable asking for help and advice.
	When this strength can be a disadvantage
	When a female manager is so calm that she does not have passion for the team accomplishments, or when she doesn't have a competitive attitude since men are known to like to compete.
Multitasking/attention to detail	Women are known to be organized and detailed and can usually handle doing a lot of things at once.
	How will this help you?
	Men prefer concise and quick actions so that they can immediately get to work creating results rather than talking in depth about the next action. Men want a leader who can catch the details that they might miss since attention to detail is not a male strength.
	When this strength can be a disadvantage
	When a female manager becomes so detailed that everything has to be done perfect. Men are often not as detail-oriented as women and will get frustrated with a lot of reworking.

Attribute	Description
Openness	Women can be open and honest and share a lot of information about tasks and results. **How will this help you?** Men respect and trust a woman manager who is open, up-front, and honest rather than a manager who keeps information to herself. **When this strength can be a disadvantage** When a female manager says too much, she can lose the respect of her male team because men can find it hard to work effectively with an overly talkative woman.
Intuition	From my experience and from the experiences of the people that I have interviewed, women can often tap into other people's needs faster and more effectively than men. Women can often pick up very subtle clues about how the people around them are feeling. **How will this help you?** Men have needs too! And those needs must be understood by their manager to ensure a productive relationship, which is something male managers aren't always as clued in to. **When this strength can be a disadvantage** When a female manager only relies on her feelings instead of actual facts and results.
Empathy	Women are often more capable than men of showing concern for other people's feelings and connecting on a personal level. **How will this help you?** Although they may not show it as easily as women, men also have feelings. Men want to be understood and supported by their manager. **When this strength can be a disadvantage** When a female manager gets too personal with non-work situations, it can make men feel uncomfortable.

After you determine what your unique leadership strengths are, brainstorm how you can use those strengths more as a manager. For instance, if you are great at listening, think about how you can meet in small groups or one-to-one with your employees to build trust on a more personal level.

 Reflection time: Before you go any further, take some time to reflect on the preceding leadership strengths and write down two strengths that you have right now. Then, write down two leadership skills that you want to improve on.

Who are your managerial role models?

Looking back at your previous managers will help you identify what type of manager you want to be. Put your previous managers' strengths and weaknesses into two categories:

➤ Strengths and weaknesses of the female managers I have had

➤ Strengths and weaknesses of the male managers I have had

My first manager, Sally, was supportive of my goals and made me feel like she always had my back. My next manager, Nancy, was always available to answer my questions and trusted me to complete tasks on my own. I was able to succeed because her delegation of tasks was organized and well thought out. My next manager, Kathy, was very understanding, and often we felt more like and friends instead of a manager and employee. She had that female intuition and knew things even before I said them.

The strengths of my previous male managers are very different. My first male manager, Anthony, used humor and jokes to break the ice. My next male manager, Timothy, was very serious, and people respected him because he was decisive and forward-thinking. But, he also intimidated a lot of people (including me). My next manager, Cory, took a hands-off approach and only checked in with me when he needed something.

My previous female managers demonstrated strengths in listening, intuition, attention to detail, and empowerment. My previous male managers demonstrated strengths such as delegation, humor, and decisiveness. These various strengths that were demonstrated to me helped me determine my managerial role models.

I hope you are seeing now that there are innate things that women, like you, excel at that men often don't, and there are some things that men excel at that women naturally don't. You have to be proud of your differences as a woman and learn to use them to build trust with your team.

Sharon Hadary, co-author of *How Women Lead: 8 Essential Strategies Successful Women Know*, said, "Don't be afraid to lead like a woman!"

Getting feedback

If something isn't going well, many managers focus on trying to improve the skills of the people they manage. Instead, self-assessment of the manager can make a big impact on the effectiveness of the team. A common saying you may have heard is that a team is only as good as its leader. You should look at yourself as a leader to see if there are any improvements you can make so your team can be more successful.

As a female manager, you want to take advantage of feedback in order to understand your current strengths and weaknesses. You want to know how people perceive you so you can have greater control of creating the outer perception that you want. The following sections mention a few ways that you can do this.

Conduct a 360 degree assessment

A 360 degree assessment is a process in which employees receive anonymous feedback from the people they work with. Create survey questions specific to your work and offer a chance to respond with numerical values such as:

"On a scale from 1 to 10, 10 being the highest, would you say your manager is supportive of your current work and future success?"

Here are some of the most popular free online options available to create your own manager assessment survey:

- Survey Monkey: http://surveymonkey.com
- Google Docs: http://docs.google.com
- 360 Degree Reach: http://www.reachcc.com/360reach

When you are done gathering feedback, don't get mad if the feedback is negative. Instead, think about how you can turn the negative response into a positive perception now that you have this information. Also, make sure you ask as many women as men for feedback to see if there are any differences in your perception based on the different genders you manage.

After you get the feedback, pick three focus areas that you are going to work on over the next year. Brainstorm action steps that you can take to improve, and focus on enhancing the positive perceptions and strengths that you already have. Mark in your calendar the actions you will take throughout the next year that will help you improve such as reading a book, taking a course, or finding a mentor.

Ask in person

Another option is to openly ask someone you currently manage in person about your management style and how you could be a better manager. This is a great way to break down any communication barriers with your team, but actually this option should not be your first choice. The employees you manage may not be completely honest with you if they are worried about getting in trouble for their feedback. The best bet is to ask for feedback anonymously.

Reflection Time: Before you go any further, take some time to write down three people that you want to ask for feedback this week.

Stop being a perfectionist

I used to drive myself crazy making sure my team's work products were 100 percent perfect for our client. Unfortunately, my team didn't have much fun working for me because I created a lot of stress. I almost had a nervous breakdown trying to keep my team operating exactly how my client wanted things to be. I didn't realize that only another woman on my team and I had this perfectionist mindset until my male manager pulled us aside one day and told both of us, "You know things don't have to be perfect."

Striving for perfection is actually one of those things that you think would be a great strength to have as a female leader, but it can be especially negative when managing men who don't have the same concern for perfection. After my male boss told me not to be perfect, I realized that men don't strive for perfection like women often do. The other woman working for me eventually moved positions, as did I, and two men took our place. They laugh, have fun, and don't stress about making things perfect. And guess what? The ship doesn't sink.

We are all imperfect, and trying to attain perfection can come with a lot of stress. Also, perfection kills creativity, which is very important when managing a team. Here are some ways you can start moving away from perfection:

- ➤ **Make a deadline for your task**: When the time comes, move on to the next task even if you haven't finished the current task. Settle for as good as can be in the time available in order not to spend countless hours trying to make it perfect. If you need to, you can always return to the task at a later time with a fresh perspective.

- ➤ **Set realistic expectations and goals**: Make sure you don't set arbitrary deadlines for yourself for no reason.

- ➤ **Ask for an extension**: I know it's hard because it shows that you aren't perfect, but usually there is no negative side-effect for asking for an extension because it shows that you really care. Just don't make a habit of constantly missing deadlines, which can ultimately ruin your trust and reputation. Make sure you know the difference between a hard deadline and a soft deadline.

How to focus on the big picture

This is another area where a positive female strength of being detail-oriented can turn into a negative quality when managing men. When my team first started working for our male client, we put together fifty page reports for him to review. He would glance at two pages and then ask us to summarize it for him. I made my team kill a few trees before I realized that our male client cared only about the "big picture" and he, like most men, was not as detail-oriented as me.

Keep a notepad next to your desk with the big picture goal that your team is trying to achieve. My team's big picture goal was to save the government money. When I started to think about telling one of the men I managed to format his Excel spreadsheets perfectly, I would look at my big picture goal and remind myself that the size of his font really doesn't matter. If you nitpick the details of a man's work product, most likely he will get frustrated with the rework, which will impact your ability to reach your big picture goal.

It is also important to think about the big picture goal when you are preparing to give a presentation. You don't need to go over all the details; just focus on what the audience really wants to know. The next time you are preparing to present something to the men you manage, think about the following:

- ➤ What do I want them to take away?
- ➤ What is the end product or the result that I want to happen?
- ➤ What is the biggest question the audience wants to know the answer to?

Don't assume that you have to present all the details to show that you know the material. Keep it short and sweet. If they want more details, they can always ask you after the presentation.

How to get over your mistakes

If you are like me, after a stupid mistake, you think about it for days and are very hard on yourself. Men often get over mistakes and losses faster than women. Researchers at the University of Waterloo in Canada found that men apologize less frequently than women because their bar for what warrants an apology is higher than for a woman. Even saying the words "I'm sorry" when, in fact, there's nothing to be sorry for is one of the 101 unconscious mistakes women make according to Lois Frankel, author of *Nice Girls Don't Get The Corner Office*. Here are some ways to get over your mistakes **fast**:

> ➤ Focus on what you did right instead of focusing on what went wrong.
> ➤ Understand why you made that mistake and figure out how not to make the same mistake again.
> ➤ Remember that mistakes can often be a good thing because you learn something from them. Think about what you learned from this mistake and move on.
> ➤ Think realistically about the mistake. Was it really **that** bad? Are you the only one who will remember it tomorrow?
> ➤ Create a new process to ensure that the mistake doesn't happen again. For example, if you forgot to complete a task, put a reminder on your c alendar for next time.

For the sake of your team, don't dwell on your team's mistakes. Start the next day fresh because you have much more important things to think about as a manager.

How to make fast decisions

As a woman in charge, you have to be able to think on your feet and take some risks. When a man you manage comes to you asking for direction, he wants a quick answer that is straight to the point. He will not be very happy with, "Well, let me think about it." Besides, it's better to delegate something to him and start him off in a direction immediately rather than you spending more of your precious time thinking about it.

Remember that something is better than nothing, and you can always make changes in the future. Here are some steps you can take to make quick decisions as a manager:

> ➤ Go with your gut. What was your first thought? Use it.
> ➤ Lay out your options. Write down the pros and cons and narrow it down.
> ➤ Lean on your previous experiences. When did you face a similar issue and what did you do?
> ➤ Don't doubt yourself. You have the knowledge and experience to make this decision, or otherwise you wouldn't have been promoted to manager. People trust you and believe you have the ability to make great decisions.

> ➤ Remove the detail and distractions. Get rid of the emotions and all other details of the decision that don't matter. What are the facts that really matter?

As a manager, you may not always know the right direction, but trust your intuition and lean on your past experiences to help you make a quick decision.

Finding your unique female leadership style

Your success as a manager depends on how confidently and comfortably you are leading. You want to be authentic and never want to act like someone you aren't. My first experience as a manager was not great, but I learned from it. I didn't get the respect I deserved from the man I managed because I was trying to be like his previous manager instead of being like myself. I was afraid of confrontation and was not comfortable leading. He could tell I was uncomfortable and he didn't respect me because of it. Little did I know he actually had a job transfer in process and already had one foot out the door!

You have to find a leadership style that works for you and believe in yourself. You don't have to become one of the guys and you don't have to fit in with everyone else. You can stand out and be different with your unique leadership style by just being yourself.

Common leadership styles

So, what type of leader are you? Daniel Goleman, author of *Primal Leadership*, describes six different styles of leadership. Answer the following questions to determine which styles reflect you most right now as a leader:

1. Do you enjoy getting your team's perspective on decisions? If so, you are a **democratic** leader.
2. Do you set high standards for your team to meet so that you can get the best possible result? If so, you are a **pacesetting** leader.
3. Do you rely on teamwork most of the time to get tasks done? Do you think two heads are better than one? If so, you are an **affiliative** leader.
4. Do you prefer to meet with your employees on an individual basis in order to discuss their development and future goals? If so, you are a **coaching** leader.
5. Do you like to envision a future goal for your team to meet? If so, you are a **visionary** leader.
6. Do you often use criticism in order to motivate your team? If so, you are a **commanding** leader. If this is you, be careful, because criticism is not usually an effective form of leadership.

The most effective female leaders can move among these styles, adopting the one that meets the needs of the moment.

What to do when....

Here are some answers to other common leadership questions:

➤ Question: How can I make sure I regularly use my leadership strengths so that I am continually improving as a manager?

Answer: Write down the strengths you already have and the characteristics you want to improve on. Review your notes on a weekly basis to see how you are doing. The best way to make sure you are on track is to continually remind yourself and assess yourself. Write down a few words that will remind you what you are working toward each month and keep the note at your desk. This visual reminder will help you remember to keep improving on a daily basis.

➤ Question: What do you do when a man resents being managed by a woman no matter what you do?

Answer: Most of the time, this is just a test of your patience and he will come around. I have had this happen, but I just kept doing what I was doing and didn't let him frustrate me. Eventually, when he saw that I knew what I was doing and that I deserved to be in a management position, he started to respect and trust me. It was just a very slow and gradual process. Stay patient and keep doing the great things you are doing; he will come around or he will quit. One way or the other, it will be OK!

Self-evaluation

Now it's time for some self-evaluation; by answering the following questions, you'll identify your knowledge of your own leadership strengths and learn to focus on what makes you unique as a female manager:

1. What are my leadership strengths and how can I use these strengths at work?
2. Do I need to focus more on the big picture and less on being a perfectionist?
3. What makes me unique as a manager?
4. What are the traits that I admire most about my previous managers?

Summary

In this chapter, you have learned:

➤ What strengths you have right now as a female manager

➤ How to get feedback to see how you are perceived as a manager

➤ How to stop being a perfectionist and focus on the big picture

➤ How to make quick decisions

➤ How to move on after a mistake

In the next chapter, you will learn how to use your strengths to communicate assertively to the men you manage.

How to Be a Confident Female Manager

In this chapter, you will learn why it is important to be self-confident when managing men and how to own the room when you walk into it. After you have read this chapter, you will be able to communicate better with the men you lead and promote yourself without being obnoxious.

We'll cover:

> How to be assertive
> How to communicate with men
> How to promote yourself without being obnoxious

Being assertive

Women are often afraid to speak up and be assertive because they don't want to hurt other people's feelings. In *Nice Girls Don't Get The Corner Office*, Lois Frankel says:

> "What women need to understand is that the fear of being seen as "not nice" or "bitchy" comes from social messages about how they should behave. The vast majority of women could be more assertive and still be far from bitchy in reality."

This chapter will teach you how to assert yourself as a smart, confident woman around the men you manage.

Why assertiveness is important

Assertiveness is an easy way to quickly gain respect from the men on your team and it can help men become more confident in you. Men respect a woman who speaks her mind and challenges others. Men want to hear your voice because you have different strengths than them and you bring a different viewpoint to the team. Men also expect interruptions because that is what they are used to when they are around other men. Therefore, your assertiveness won't be seen as overbearing (or bitchy!).

When you waver or ask for reassurance, you lose trust and respect. If you sweat, your team sweats. If you simply go along with what other people say, you lose credibility.

There is a woman that I work with who intimidates men because of how assertive she is in meetings. Even though the men are scared of her, they also respect her because she asks intelligent questions and knows her stuff. She is not afraid to challenge a man, is focused on her big picture goal, and never backs down.

On the other hand, I also work with a woman who is very assertive but asks dumb questions. She has lost respect from all of the men she works with because of her lack of understanding. Be aware that being assertive isn't the only goal; it is being assertive *and* smart.

How to be assertive AND smart

You have to act self-confident even if you aren't really feeling it. If you aren't confident in yourself, why should anyone else believe you? According to Dr. Valerie Young, author of *The Secret Thoughts of Successful Women: Why Capable Women Suffer from the Impostor Syndrome and How to Thrive in Spite of It*, says that women need to:

> "Make it a skill to wing it."

Here are some ways that you can be assertive AND smart:

> ➤ Gather as much information as possible before a meeting so that you have all your thoughts ready to present.

> ➤ Practice role-playing with a friend or co-worker beforehand.

> ➤ Don't wait for an opportunity to talk. Practice being the first to speak.

> ➤ Start small. Practice being assertive by asking for that discount on your grocery bill. Once you succeed, you will be more confident the next time you challenge someone.

> ➤ Asking a question is an easy way to assert yourself because it usually doesn't make the other person feel bad.

> ➤ Identify the situations where you will most likely have trouble speaking up. Think about what you want to say and why you are scared to say it. Then, think of what the worst thing is that could happen if you say it. You probably have nothing to lose.

> ➤ Instead of telling someone that you think they are wrong, try offering suggestions to soften the blow.

Whatever you do, think about the big picture goal. If you hurt someone's feelings, it might last for a day or two, but your big picture goal is what is most important. Besides, most men get over things a lot faster than women.

How to set your limits

Setting your limits from day one as a manager will help you to stay assertive. You want to communicate your expectations on day one because then you and your employees are all on the same page. You can then be assertive if someone doesn't perform up to your expectations.

I teach a career development course for college students and I set my expectations on the first day of class. When a student tries to submit a late assignment a few weeks into the course, I can be assertive and say that I don't accept late assignments according to the expectations we went over the first night in class. Without those expectations being delivered up front, I would not have any ground to stand on to assert myself and my requirements.

Here are some ways to set your limits as a manager:

> ➤ If you are starting with a new team, set up a meeting to introduce yourself and let them know your expectations on the very first day.

> ➤ If you have a new person entering your team, hold a one-to-one meeting with them as soon as possible to communicate your expectations.

> ➤ Have a written document that a new employee has to review that clearly outlines your requirements so that you can always reference it if there are questions.

If you don't communicate what you expect from your team from the beginning, it will be harder to communicate with a male employee if he doesn't do something the way you like. Men will respond better when they know the instructions they should follow. Set your limits from the beginning and you will be able to assert yourself more easily.

How to assert yourself physically

Did you know that you can assert yourself around men without even saying a word? You can actually assert yourself just by your presence when entering a room.

Your goal is to be noticed when you walk into a room; not for being attractive, but for being well put together professionally so you demand respect. Here are some ways that you can assert yourself without saying a word:

- Pay attention to your posture. Keep your back straight and head up. You want to be seen as equal to a man.

- Don't cross your arms because it will make you appear angry. Instead, keep your arms open so you look approachable.

- Don't play with your hair. This bad habit is foreign to men and it will make you look like a nervous young girl.

- Before you walk into a room, pause and take a deep breath. Think about how you want to show confidence from the second you enter the room. On a scale of 1 to 10, with 10 being the very best, you want to be a 10 the entire time that you are in that room.

- Make sure your dress is professional and appropriate at all times. According to Sarah Ward, owner of Cable Car Couture Image Consulting,

  "One thing every professional woman needs to have in her wardrobe is a blazer or jacket. Someone wearing a blazer is going to hold someone's attention longer and is going to appear more credible."

- Look directly in the eyes of the person who is speaking. Never be distracted by your phone or papers. Remember, men want to be listened to.

- Practice active listening by making mental points in your head while someone is speaking. You want to make sure that you have an opinion when the person speaking is done presenting. If you have a hard time remembering, take notes on what you want to say when the presentation is over.

Once you discover how to assert yourself physically, you may be surprised at the attention you receive. I often receive a "Good morning Anna", whereas a man who entered may just receive a nod. This makes it easier to ask a question or make a comment because I was already noticed when I walked in.

How to be tough and not overbearing

Most likely, you are a long way from being overbearing. But, there are some things you want to watch out for when being tough and assertive:

- Never be confrontational, argumentative, or rude.

- Never accuse anyone, interrupt anyone, or talk down to anyone.

- If you feel yourself getting angry, take a five-minute break to cool off. Try your hardest to listen to what others are saying at all times.

Always be patient and respectful, as respect is the one thing that you should stay focused on when challenging others. When someone challenges me disrespectfully, I shut down, and you can't let that happen with the men on your team. Value all of the voices in the room because if employees are scared of you, they won't want to speak up and you will miss out on their great ideas.

Communicating with men

One of the biggest mistakes a female manager can make is to communicate with a man the same way she would communicate with a woman. Your speaking style really needs to change depending on who you are talking to. But don't worry; it really is quite simple to communicate with a man. When you are speaking to a male employee, keep it short and sweet. If you can reduce the time you spend in the conversation and get to the point as quickly as possible, the more success you will have.

For example, I once managed a woman who presented a report to our male client by providing all of the background information first. The client didn't even let her finish before he started giving negative feedback. I had to quickly jump in and provide the main point, which she had not communicated yet, at which point he was much happier.

The most successful women at my company know exactly how to do this. When you have a meeting with them, you know what they want in the first minute, and then we get straight to the point of the meeting. This also means that you don't have to have long-drawn-out meetings. You can accomplish the most in a short amount of time if you focus on what is important, and only that.

How to get straight to the point

Cutting to the chase quickly is really important when managing men. Imagine that there is a man and a woman giving a presentation about how to increase sales at their company. To introduce her strategy, a woman says:

> *"I know that this is a really tough year for our company and we all want to figure out how to increase sales so that we don't lose our jobs. Well, I have spent a lot of time researching the problem and coming up with a solution, and I would like to share my strategy with you today."*

To introduce the same strategy, a man says:

> *"I have done research on this problem and here is the solution that I see."*

Do you see how the man introduces the subject and gets right to the point? The woman gets to the point at the end but it takes a while to get there. It's important to note that women in the audience may appreciate the woman's introduction. But, the men in the audience might be tuning her out by the time she actually gets to the point.

Cutting to the chase quickly is really important when managing men. Here are some ways you can get straight to the point:

> ➤ Before you talk with a male employee, plan out what you are going to say. If you are worried about it being lengthy, write it down and make sure it is concise. What are the facts you need to communicate? That is all they care about.

> ➤ Keep the stories to a minimum. You don't want their mind to wander, and saying too much can cause them to stop listening.

> ➤ When you are done making your point, show interest in what they think by asking direct questions such as, "Does that make sense?" or "What do you think?" Make sure that you ask whether they understand, and be willing to explain it further if needed.

> ➤ If you don't have anything to say, end the meeting. I have never heard a complaint that a meeting ended early. Have you?

It's not hard to be concise, it just takes preparation. My dad recently taught me the **KISS** method—**Keep It Simple, Stupid**. Remember this method the next time you speak to a man on your team.

How to make your voice heard

A louder voice communicates that you have confidence in yourself and you know what you are talking about. Unfortunately, women are often at a disadvantage because we normally have softer voices than men. There is one thing that I learned quickly when working around a lot of men—how to raise my voice. You often have to speak louder than you might think is normal and you can't be afraid of speaking too loud. It's almost impossible to speak too loud in a group of men.

Here are some questions to think about:

> ➤ Is it common for people to ask you to repeat what you said?

> ➤ Have people told you that you speak too softly?

> ➤ Do you feel like you can't compete with the loud male voices on your team?

 One quick way to find out if you are speaking too softly is to ask other people.

Here are some ways you can project your voice when speaking:

> ➤ Stand up straight with your head high. Try to relax your neck and shoulders while speaking.

> ➤ Prepare beforehand and be confident in your material. People really want to hear what you have to say, so say it with confidence. If you have worked hard to prepare and practice, you will be great!

> ➤ Think positively, not negatively. Imagine yourself nailing it.

> ➤ Speaking from your stomach makes your voice louder. Get your whole body into it and project that voice.

> ➤ Practice makes perfect. You can train yourself to speak louder as long as you keep practicing. I used to be the shy girl. Now I give presentations to hundreds of people who tell me that I am a great presenter. How did I change? For many years, I practised practicing speaking up and raising my voice so that it was stronger.

> ➤ Take deep breaths to allow for a stronger voice. When you forget to breathe, your voice will get really soft.

When speaking on the phone, you only have your voice to build trust and communicate what you know. One day, I overheard a man telling a woman that he could barely hear her on the teleconference. He said, "Speak up next time!" You can never be too loud over the phone and your loud phone voice is still quieter than a man's normal phone voice. Next time you are on the phone, speak even louder than you think is normal.

Promoting yourself

Most women are more comfortable being humble and not attracting attention. They believe other people will know how awesome they are without them having to say it. Women have often not been raised to self-promote. When I was growing up, my dad would brag about the things I was doing to other people and I would get so embarrassed (I still sometimes do).

Men, on the other hand, are often naturals at promoting themselves to others, and it is fairly common for them to promote themselves in a group of men.

If you did a great thing, say it. Don't wait to be called on or until it is your turn. More than likely, the men on your team want to hear how awesome you are. They want to be proud of their manager and your big wins and victories. They will respect you if you show that you are worthy of that respect. You are invited into the club of bragging and self-promotion. Will you accept the invitation?

Show how awesome you are!

One day at work, I received two e-mails. One was from a man on my team and one was from a woman. I had congratulated the woman on an award that her team had just received. In response to my e-mail, she said, "Oh, that award wasn't for me. I wasn't even here when that award was written up." She missed her chance to say, "Thanks! Yes, I have been working my butt off here and I am doing a great job!" She made herself look less than the awesome and hard-working person that I know she is.

On the other hand, the e-mail I received from the man said, "Look at this awesome thing that I was able to complete!" He had finally completed something that he had not been able to do for the past year. He sent that e-mail to our entire team to brag about his accomplishment. I congratulated him and said, "Wow, that is awesome! Good for you!" In my eyes, unfortunately, the man scored some points that day and the woman lost some points for not promoting herself.

Here are some ways that you can spread the news about how awesome you are:

➤ Take this sentence out of your vocabulary: "Oh, it's no big deal." Be proud of your accomplishments and say thank you when someone says "Good job!"

➤ If you have a great thing that you know you did, just say it. Don't wait for someone to call on you or for someone else to discover it.

➤ Get in the habit of sharing e-mails about good work or presenting good news during team meetings.

➤ Send thank you notes to honor the work that other people in your office are doing. What goes around comes around. Your team will soon start sharing and complimenting you on your work as well.

➤ Look for ways to expand your skills and knowledge by attending classes, reading books, and attending conferences. Then, don't be afraid to tell the team what you are learning and working on.

➤ Find ways to get what you and your team are doing into the press. Write blogs, e-mails, and articles about the accomplishments your team is achieving and send them to your management. If you learn how to promote yourself and your team, your team will be proud to work for you.

➤ Build a rapport with your team before you start promoting yourself. You want to develop those relationships and connections first before you start bragging.

Constantly build up your reputation by sharing what you are doing to build respect for you and your work. If you have a great thing that you know you did, just say it.

How to toot your own horn without being obnoxious

There is a fine line between respectful self-promotion and obnoxious self-promotion. If you over-promote your abilities and accomplishments, you will lose respect instead of gaining respect. In order to make it appear that you aren't just bragging about yourself, here are some things that you can do:

➤ Use the KISS principle (Keep It Simple Stupid). Promote the result that you helped make happen. You don't have to keep talking about how you made it happen and lose their respect with a long drawn-out story.

➤ Ask questions to hear about the awesome things that the other person is doing as well. Give them praise too.

➤ Don't change the conversation drastically so you can brag. Wait for a time when it comes up naturally in the conversation.

➤ Never lie. Don't make it appear better than it really is.

➤ Think about subtle ways you can inform others of your accomplishments such as forwarding an e-mail or an online article about yourself.

You can promote yourself and you don't have to be sleazy to do it. Congratulations! You now have permission to go and inform others of your great accomplishments!

Self-evaluation

Now it's time for some self-evaluation; by answering the following questions, you'll identify your knowledge of how to communicate with the men you manage and help you establish their trust:

1. How can I be more assertive at work?
2. How can I physically assert myself when I walk into a room?
3. How can I better communicate with the men on my team?
4. What are some things that hold me back from being assertive and speaking out?
5. How can I promote myself more at work?

Summary

In this chapter, you learned:

➤ How to be assertive AND smart

➤ How to be tough but not overbearing

➤ How to communicate with men and get straight to the point

➤ How to speak out with a strong voice

In the next chapter, you will learn how to support the men on your team and how to embrace their love of competition and sense of humor.

>3

How to Help the Men on Your Team Thrive

In this chapter, you will learn how to use men's love for competition and gamesmanship for the benefit of your team. After you have read this chapter, you will be able to use humor to your advantage and coach the men you manage to be all that they are capable of.

We'll cover:

- ➤ How to embrace men's love for competition
- ➤ How to use humor to lighten things up
- ➤ How to do office sports talk
- ➤ How to build trust with the men you manage
- ➤ How to coach the men on your team

Embracing the competition

It's no secret that men like to compete. You can even trace the role of competition in a man's upbringing back to his childhood. Think back to the boys on the playground showing off and competing for that popular girl's attention. In *Women Don't Ask*, authors Sara Laschever and Linda Babcock say:

> *"Boys learn that they are expected to compete, that being a good competitor is a defining male trait."*

Now the boy is all grown up, but he still thrives on competition. The trick as a manager is to use his love of competition to drive your team as a whole forward, instead of the men on your team competing *against* you. This chapter will teach you how to make man's love of gamesmanship work for you.

How to successfully compete with men

It's very obvious when it's football season in my office. The fantasy football scorecard poster is on the wall. The morning sports talk consists of a recap of the winners and losers of the week. Replays of game-winning plays are shown over and over again during the lunch break. Yes, as women working with men, we have all been there. One thing I have noticed is that whether or not they win or lose, they *really* enjoy the competition.

A common mistake I have seen women make is to distance themselves from the competition and the sports talk in the office. If you do this, you will be left out of the opportunities to build relationships with the men on your team. You will also miss out on the chance to get to know the men on your team on a more competitive and fun level. Also, if you understand how they compete, you can understand their behavior better in the office. In my research for this book, I interviewed a male CEO, and he said:

> *"Watching how someone plays golf can tell you a lot. Will they lie and cheat? Do they play fair? Do they keep a cool head? Do they get frustrated easily? Do they have good etiquette? These are the things you want to know."*

 The way I have see competition in my office – get involved or get left out.

Here are some ways to embrace the male competition in your office:

> Don't shy away from conflict. Get used to debate. Make conflict productive by getting all ideas out on the table and have everyone share what they think is the best option.

> Men often put more on the line for that big goal and so should you. As long as you don't put everything on the line, get used to going with your gut and being a risk-taker.

> Men don't often take losses personally and neither should you. Move on and do better the next time because tomorrow is a new day.

> ➤ Find your game face. Look at a picture of a male sports star and see how tough he looks on the outside. That's how men approach competition; you should have the same intensity (with a little class of course).

> ➤ Always be on the lookout for a new opportunity. When you are given new opportunities, take them without hesitation.

> ➤ Always remember good sportsman-like behavior. You *never* want to take competition too far to the point it becomes disrespectful or uncomfortable for you or your employees.

As a female manager, the best way to compete *with* men instead of *against* men is to:

- ■ Never say no to a challenge or competition that a man on your team proposes
- ■ Find ways to start challenges and competitions for your team

How to make competition work for your team

Your goal is to make men's love of competition work positively for your entire team. You should create opportunities for your employees to cooperatively compete with each other even if your current work environment is non-competitive. Competition can help men excel beyond what they or even you thought possible. You should push them, which will often lead to higher-quality work.

In *Chapter 1, Focus on You First*, you learned that one of our strengths as women is being able to build a team that collaborates together. Use this strength to build a collaborative team that competes *with* each other to make the team, as a whole, better. Take the male competitiveness on your team and use it to reach your vision.

Here is how to make competition work for your team of men:

> ➤ Create a competition and offer a prize for the winner. Even if it is a $5 Starbucks gift card, it will get the men's competitive juices flowing. You could also have happy hours or events for the winning teams. Or, you could say that the prize will be a surprise (which will give you some time to think about it).

> ➤ Create a competition where everyone on your team is working toward the same goal. This will help your team bond and encourage each other to reach the final goal together.

> ➤ Create a way to track the team's success such as putting updates on a wall or sending e-mail updates so that everyone can stay involved and excited.

It's easy (and boring) to come to work every day and do the same job without an incentive. Make it fun for your male employees to meet your vision for your team with a little friendly competition.

How to do office sports talk

A study of Harvard Business School graduates found that 85 percent of the time, men initiated sports talk, not women (not a shocker, I know). If you work in an environment where men constantly talk about sports, you aren't alone.

 While presenting my book topic of managing men with a group of male and female MBA students, I heard from a woman that she claimed her success in the workforce was primarily due to the fact that she watched 30 minutes of ESPN every morning.

Here are some tips on how to *not* be an outsider during sports talk:

> Skim the online sports page or watch the sports highlights before you head to work. If you know everyone in your office will be talking about the Superbowl on a Monday morning, at least catch some of the highlights of the game (and the half-time show).

> Don't block out the sports talk voices going on around you. You have to at least know what is going on and who is winning and losing. Join in with the fun and encourage the loser or say good job to the winner. This is a great way to stay involved but not actually be competing yourself.

> Make sure you catch up on the big news stories that will be talked about for years to come, for example, the Tiger Woods infidelity scandal, the Janet Jackson Superbowl wardrobe malfunction, and so on.

> If there is a competition going on, ask to join. Even if you don't know all the rules of the game, you will learn while playing. You never know, you might kick their butts! From what I hear, most games like Fantasy Football are based on luck anyway. The guys on your team will probably be excited that you asked to join in. Who doesn't want to beat their boss? (I am already cheering you on!)

> If sports talk in the office annoys you, change your mindset. If the men on your team are talking sports, most likely that means they like each other and *enjoy* coming to work. It is a very positive thing if your employees are happy.

 Make sure that you only participate in what you are comfortable with. For me, I am not comfortable going on a two-hour lunch break to watch soccer games every week or drinking beer with a bunch of guys during Monday night football at a bar. That is OK!

Using humor

In my work as a consultant, I work with men in the military. They have a habit of saying things they find funny but are often rude. I always keep my professional poise but I am not afraid to dish out a joke or two if needed. This has helped me maintain a fun and friendly relationship with my male clients because they see that I am not serious all the time and I do have a sense of humor. Often, women are afraid to use humor in the office because they fear it will be unprofessional, but don't be afraid to throw out a joke so that you can create a relationship with the men on your team that is fun and enjoyable.

Why humor is important

When my husband first met me, I was so nervous that I didn't laugh at any of his jokes. He wrote me off that day because he didn't think I had a sense of humor. Thankfully, I laughed at his jokes the second time I saw him, and the third time, and so on.

In *A Woman's Guide to Successful Negotiating*, authors Lee E. Miller and Jessica Miller say:

> *"Humor is used when you negotiate, not just to get a laugh, but also to ease the tension. Having a sense of humor makes people want to be around you. Humor enables you to connect with someone on a personal level and show him or her another side of you."*

Men in my office use humor as a way to get through a stressful day. As women, we tend to err on the side of professionalism and less on the side of joking around. But, it's important for us to make sure that we don't stay serious all the time and that we show we can take a little break as well. We need to show our sense of humor in order to maintain a fun and friendly relationship with the men that we work with. If the men who work for you don't see you pausing to take a break or to laugh occasionally, they won't have any fun coming to work.

How to use humor with the men you manage

The men I work with have a swear jar, and every time someone swears, they have to deposit money into the jar. They couldn't care less what the end prize is or whether they win or lose, they just *love* having this friendly competition going on every day. Now, as Classy Career Girl, of course I would never swear at work. But, I still want to join in on this friendly competition with the men. So, I join in as a monitor, and when I hear a swear word, I make sure that they pay up. Even though their game might be a *man's game*, I am still getting involved and sharing in the humor with the men on my team.

> *"The most wasted of all days is one without laughter."*
>
> —E.E. Cummings

Most of us spend at least forty hours a week with the people we work with, and it is OK to lighten up and enjoy being around each other. Remember that happy men are more motivated and productive at work.

Here is how to use humor with the men you manage:

> ➤ Don't worry about always being the first one to crack a funny joke. You don't have to be a comedian. You can show that you have a sense of humor just by laughing at someone else's jokes.
>
> ➤ Use humor when things are tense to diffuse the situation. If you can sense an argument coming, try to lighten the mood so that the men on your team don't get aggressive or angry.
>
> ➤ Don't be afraid to laugh at yourself if you did something silly or stupid.

➤ Stay with positive humor, not negative humor. It's never OK to make discriminating or disrespectful jokes. Humor should never make people feel uncomfortable. It if does, you are doing it wrong.

➤ Create a bulletin board with funny sayings your employees said or funny things that happened in the office. This will make your team of men smile when they see it.

➤ Office pranks are totally allowed. My favorites have to do with post-it notes and screensavers. Just don't go overboard.

➤ Learn comedic timing. If there is a deadline that your team has to meet in an hour, save your joke for later on in the day.

➤ I will tell you a little secret: men want to be told that they are funny. This is one of the greatest compliments that you can give to a guy. If you think a man on your team is funny, tell him.

> *"Life is relationships. The rest is just details."*

> —*Gary Smalley*

Helping men get to the top

Men are outcome-focused and goal-oriented. According to Sara Laschever, co-author of *Women Don't Ask* and *Ask For It*:

> *"Since boys were little, they have been trying to figure out how to reach their goals. Boys desire certain toys that will help them meet their end goal. Toys for boys are all about meeting goals such as a tunnel on the train tracks or a toy truck to reach the end of the driveway. On the other hand, toys for girls are about helping others such as a doll or a cooking set."*

Because men are competitive, they will want to know how they are doing and what they can do better to reach their goals. To build trust, you should show the men you manage that you want to help them on their path to reach their goals.

How to build trust with men

Trust is vital to the communication and success of your team. A survey by Development Dimensions International found that 99 percent of employees think trust in the workplace is a vital need at work, but only 29 percent reported a high level of trust within their organization.

Here are some ways that you can build trust with your team:

> ➤ Men want to work for someone who is knowledgeable and experienced, so don't be afraid to share your knowledge and experiences with the men you manage. Help them become better by sharing what you already know so they don't make the same mistakes you did.

> ➤ Care about your employees. Men don't show their feelings as much as women, but they still want to be cared for. Be there for them when they have a question. Always listen to them and let them know that you genuinely care about their thoughts and feelings.

> ➤ Be truthful and transparent. Never keep things to yourself and always be open with the men you work with. Men will trust a manager who is open and honest.

> ➤ Take responsibility if something is your fault. Men will trust a woman who is willing to acknowledge her faults and correct them.

If you continue to do these steps over and over again, the trust will come as you show consistency. Men may not open up right away and share their thoughts and feelings, and you might find them very hard to read at first. It may take more time for men to develop their trust in you, but it will come with time. If you want to get to know them on a more personal level, don't bug them with personal questions. Just build the trust first.

How to coach and support men

After you build trust, think of your job as manager like that of a coach of a sports team. You are the coach and the men you manage are the athletes. You are going to coach them to reach the top of their game.

Here are some ways that you can coach and support the men on your team:

> ➤ Men want feedback, but because of the difference in genders, they might not ask a woman for feedback as quickly as they might ask a man for feedback. Tell him how he can improve and then watch him get better. Make sure you give both positive and negative feedback.

> ➤ Push them to reach their fullest potential. A little challenge will get their competitive juices flowing. Try saying:

> > *"Do you think you can do better?"*

> ➤ Be honest and don't sugar-coat anything. Tell it like it is (quickly and concisely, remember what you learned in the previous chapter).

> ➤ Always find time to answer their questions.

> ➤ Don't micromanage.

> > *"If your actions inspire others to dream more, learn more, do more, and become more, you are a leader."*

> > —*John Quincy Adams*

What to do when...

Here are some answers to some common leadership questions:

➤ Question: What should you do if you want to include competition within your team but the women are turned off by work-based competitions?

Answer: Women can feel different than men about a friendly competition. From my experience, it usually just takes one quick game to get her away from worrying about her workload to see how fun it is. But, it could be that the women on your team don't feel comfortable competing with men. If there is a woman on your team who doesn't want to join in on the fun, I would speak with her individually so you can identify *why* she doesn't want to participate. Once you have that conversation, tell her your reasons for using competition on your team (you should also give her this book so she can understand how to work with men better!) Ask her to help you and to try it out. Then, check in on her throughout the competition.

➤ Question: I don't think I am that funny, so how can I respond to and create humorous situations at work? What are some examples that I can use?

Answer: First, make sure that you are smiling and laughing at other situations that come up. Then, don't be afraid to poke fun at yourself for the funny things that you have done as well. It is OK to make yourself the punch-line because it shows that you don't take yourself that seriously. Now, before you think you have to share your most embarrassing moment, try sharing those stupid little situations like knocking over the trash can or tripping over the carpet. If you do something funny in the office, make light of it. Men do this *all the time*. Last week in the office, a man on my team made himself the punch-line by telling us that he saw one of the executives at my company at Starbucks. After he said hello to him, he spilled his coffee all over himself. He could have kept this very embarrassing situation to himself, but instead he chose to tell everyone in the office and laugh at himself with the rest of the team.

Self-evaluation

Now it's time for some self-evaluation; by answering the following questions, you'll identify your knowledge of how to use competition and humor with the men you manage to develop trust and a more successful team.

Here are some questions to answer about what you learned in this chapter. Try to think of three answers for each question and then check back through the chapter to see if you answered them correctly:

1. How can I compete *with* the men I manage, instead of *against* the men I manage?

2. How can I use men's love of competition to help my team become more successful?

3. How can I handle office sports talk as a manager?

4. How can I build trust with the men I manage?

5. How can I support and coach the men I manage?

Summary

In this chapter, you learned:

➤ How to successfully compete *with* men, not *against* men

➤ How to make competition work for your team's success

➤ How to create a relationship with the men you manage that is fun and enjoyable

➤ Actions you can do to develop trust with the men on your team

➤ How to coach the men on your team to reach the top of their game

In the next chapter, you will learn what *not* to do when managing men to ensure that you continue to build the trust and respect you deserve.

>4

What NOT To Do When Managing Men

In this chapter, you will learn about some of the common mistakes female managers make when managing men, including getting too personal, becoming the "office mom" and getting into office relationships. After you read this chapter, you will know what you might be doing subconsciously while managing men that could be harmful to your future success. Most men you manage want to be respectful, but these mistakes can make it hard for them to respect you because they feel uncomfortable.

We'll cover:

- ➤ How to not get too personal at work with men
- ➤ How to not play the role of "office mom"
- ➤ How to draw the line with office relationships

Getting too personal with men you manage

Men and women are wired differently. Most men like to maintain a distance between their work lives and personal lives. In my research for this book, I asked a man if he ever experienced his female manager getting too personal with him. He told me he once asked his female manager if he could get her some coffee. She told him that she couldn't drink coffee because she had cysts in her breasts. He immediately was uncomfortable and thought it was an inappropriate conversation for the workplace because it didn't affect work at all (couldn't she have just said she couldn't drink coffee for health reasons instead of saying the B word in the office?!).

 I have heard women in my office come in on Monday morning sharing that they were still hungover from playing beer games on Saturday night. Keep your distance from sharing personal details about your weekend to gain and keep respect from the men on your team.

Why it is important to keep some distance

Men like to be in control and when you bring up personal items, it can make them feel out of control and vulnerable. Even though you spend at least eight hours a day, five days a week with the men you manage (maybe even more time than you do with your family), you have to maintain some level of privacy.

 You are working with men, not women. They are different and handle things differently. Revealing too much personal information may give men the wrong impression about you. You should keep a certain level of privacy and not pry into their personal lives either.

How to keep your distance

When I went through a tough personal situation, I didn't want to talk about it at work. Work was a time when I didn't have to think about my personal situation and what was going wrong at home. I also didn't want my personal situation to interfere with my job. With a man, this avoidance of personal problems can be even more extreme at work since men are known to *not* want to show their emotions. Men can be worried that they are being judged if they say how they feel to their female manager.

Here are some things to remember when keeping your distance with the men you manage:

➤ Men may open up in time if they want to, but *never* force them to open up to you. If your male employee is going through a difficult tough situation, respect him. Offer your sympathy, but don't pry into his personal life.

➤ Before you say something personal about yourself, think about whether it affects your work. If not, don't say it. Be yourself, but set boundaries. No one in the office needs to know all your personal business.

➤ Be careful with the questions you ask the men you manage. Since you are an authority figure, men might feel uncomfortable saying that they don't feel comfortable answering your questions.

> ➤ Remember that how you phrase questions is really important. For example, you should say, "How was your weekend?" rather than "What did you and your wife do this weekend?"

 A general rule: If what you are going to say has to do with tampons, childbirth, or breasts, don't say it!

Playing "office mom"

It's our nature as women to want to take care of others. We want other people to like us and men sure do like us when we bring them food! But, it's important to draw a line between you as a woman in the office and you as a woman at home. Do you want to be known as the smart manager who rocks at leading the team? Or do you want to be known as the lady who makes some mean chocolate chip cookies just like mom used to make? Cooking and cleaning up for the office in the role of "office mom" is not the answer to get people to *like* you as a manager. You want people to like you for the strengths that you bring as a manager (which you learned in *Chapter 1, Focus on You First*).

Why playing "office mom" is a major no

In *Nice Girls Don't Get the Corner Office: 101 Unconscious Mistakes Women Make That Sabotage Their Careers*, author Lois Frankel says:

> *"Mistake #27: Feeding others. You're not "Mom" or Betty Crocker."*

Lois Frankel says feeding others in the office will prevent them from seeing you as a figure of authority.

Not once in seven years working in a corporate environment have I ever seen a man bring in food he made to share. I have seen men bring in food that their wives have made, but *never* food that they actually made themselves. It just doesn't happen. That is why I have never brought food I made into the office either. Don't get me wrong, I love to cook and you can find me in my kitchen cooking most nights of the week. But, when managing men, I don't want to lose my authority by bringing them coffee and donuts. I don't want to lose any respect as a confident female leader or have them think of me any differently because I clean up after them. And, I sure don't want to be taken advantage of.

How to NOT play "office mom"

Here are some ways that you can make sure you don't become the "office mom":

> ➤ Refrain from using the term "boy" when referring to men. No man likes to be called a boy because it makes him look less masculine.

> ➤ Don't bring in food that you made at home unless it is your own lunch.

> ➤ If you must have a candy jar on your desk, use it *only* to encourage others to come to your desk to communicate with you.

> ➤ Don't nag. Remember how you hated it when your mom told you to clean up your room? Telling a man the same thing over and over again will start to annoy him just like his mother once did.

> ➤ Always keep your office decorations professional. Your office should be comfortable for a man and should not look like your living room or bedroom.

> ➤ After an office party, make sure *everyone* cleans up afterwards, not just the women. If you must pitch in, make sure the men are tasked to help as well remember that you are the manager; make the men clean up too!

> ➤ Your kitchen is at home. Don't spend hours in the work kitchen. Get in and get out.

 Keeping your distance from the role of "office mom" will maintain your position of authority over the men you manage.

Office relationships

As a manager, do you want to be known as a confident and smart female manager who makes good decisions? Or do you want to be the center of the office gossip for dating a man that you manage and making questionable decisions in your personal life? If you ask me, I want to be known for my brain and *not* who I kissed last night.

I do know a couple that started a relationship in the office and eventually got married. But, it was difficult for them to keep it a secret and one of them had to eventually leave the firm. Gossip and rumors can start quickly so you have to draw a hard line fast. If someone feels that you are showing favoritism to the man you are romantically involved with, it can get real tricky, real fast. Resentment from others and tense situations are right around the corner. You have to stay true to who you are and the values that you have. And of course, always stay classy.

> *"Always be classy. Never be crazy."*

—Greg Behrendt

How to draw the line with office relationships

Here are some ways to stay away from office relationships as a manager:

> ➤ Know the risks. Starting a relationship with a man that you manage is off limits because it's too risky for your professional future.

> ➤ Don't even think that you are going to be able to hide an office relationship. You won't be able to hide it for very long and you definitely want to be ahead of the gossip curve. People that you work with all day, every day are smarter than you think (some of them will change their job to office spy if you aren't careful).

➤ When you are on business travel, you don't need to be out of your hotel room late. Nothing good ever happens after 7 p.m. when you are traveling for business. (Also, nothing good ever happens when you are intoxicated…try sticking to a two-drink maximum. Just because it is expensed on the company card doesn't mean you need to go all out).

➤ Be aware of one-on-one meetings with the men you manage at restaurants and coffee shops. These can quickly turn into "date" types of situations. Try to bring along another work colleague to these meetings. Try to hold the meeting in the office or where there will be a lot of people around. If you need to leave the office, recommend breakfast or lunch meetings over happy hours and dinners. You don't want a business meeting to turn into an uncomfortable situation.

➤ Make it easy for the men you work with by *never* dressing provocatively. You want to be known for your brains, not for your cleavage or your nice legs.

➤ In *Chapter 2, How To Be a Confident Female Manager*, you learned how to keep a sense of humor with the men you work with. But, it's important to stand up for yourself if you are receiving sexist jokes or comments. You don't have to take harassment. Don't be afraid to report something if it makes you feel uncomfortable.

 Having an office relationship is way too dangerous. Don't play with fire because it can backfire and ruin the professional reputation that you have worked so hard to create.

Self-evaluation

Now it's time for some self-evaluation. By answering the following questions, you'll reaffirm your knowledge of common mistakes that female managers make and how to avoid them.

1. Am I too personal with what I share at work?

    ➤ Do I make men uncomfortable?

    ➤ Am I careful and cautious about the questions that I ask men?

2. Do I ever ask my male employees personal questions?

    ➤ Do I force men to open up and share personal things with me?

    ➤ What might I be doing subconsciously that could be damaging the respect I want to receive as a female manager?

3. Are there any areas where I am currently playing "office mom"?

    ➤ Do I end up cleaning after office lunches and parties?

    ➤ Do I bring in food and drinks that I make for the men on my team?

    ➤ Is my office decorated like my bedroom?

4. What can I do to ensure that I stay away from an office relationship?

    ➤ Do I make appropriate decisions regarding office relationships?

    ➤ Do I dress professionally or provocatively at work?

Summary

In this chapter, you learned:

> ➤ Why you should keep your distance and not get too personal
>
> ➤ How to maintain your distance from the role of "office mom"
>
> ➤ The risks of office relationships and how to draw the line

In the next chapter, you will learn etiquette tips for specific management situations that you will most likely encounter when managing men.

>5

Handling Common Male Management Situations

In this chapter, you will learn how to handle common management situations that you will most likely encounter when managing men. As we have seen in previous chapters, men often think and communicate differently to women, which is why you should be prepared to conduct management situations differently. After you read this chapter, you will be prepared to successfully handle common management situations.

We'll cover:

- ➤ How to provide feedback to men
- ➤ How to handle social events with men
- ➤ How to negotiate with men

How to give feedback to men

Knowing how men communicate and receive feedback can help you avoid misunderstandings. Women are less confrontational than men and are often more concerned about hurting others' feelings. Women tend to "beat around the bush" instead of going head on with feedback they need to deliver.

 You cannot avoid or tiptoe around giving the feedback that men on your team need to hear.

In my research for this book, I spoke to a man who had a negative experience during a performance review with his female manager. He walked into the meeting thinking that he was doing quite well, but his manager dropped a bomb on him. After some casual small talk about other topics, she proceeded by telling him everything he had been doing wrong over the entire last year. He was in total shock because she had not given him any previous feedback and he was now receiving it all at once.

He really wished she had given him ongoing feedback so that he would know how he could have improved, and had an opportunity to improve before the annual performance review. Looking back, he knew it was because the manager was afraid to hurt his feelings or their relationship.

 Don't sugarcoat it. Give informal and honest feedback on a daily basis instead of having it boil up inside of you and exploding in an annual performance review.

A 7-step feedback model for women managing men

It can be intimidating for a woman to provide feedback to a man. Men may not be as quick to solicit feedback from a woman and they definitely don't enjoy being criticized, especially by a woman. This can make giving feedback to a man a little tricky. Men are also less likely to ask for validation and positive reinforcement than women. I spoke with a man who rarely asks for feedback from his manager. He said:

> "I rarely ask for feedback because I always assume I am doing it right unless feedback is given to me. I also don't usually want to hear the feedback if I am doing it wrong, which is why I sometimes avoid asking for it."

Because of men's confidence in themselves, constructive feedback should be an ongoing process, not a once a year event. You need to make sure that you are vocal about what you expect so that your male employees can meet or exceed your expectations.

Next time you need to give feedback to a man on your team, use this 7-step model:

1. Prepare in advance to provide feedback. Make sure you have thought of an example and action step that you can provide him with when you speak to him.

2. Ask your male employee if he has a minute for you to provide some quick feedback. He will be less likely to get defensive if you ask for permission ahead of time.

3. State specific examples to him that you observed without being judgmental. For example, "I noticed the report you submitted to our client had some grammar mistakes."

4. Explain why this impacts you or your team's performance. Be as specific as you can and include measurable impacts as evidence if possible. For example, "One of the errors I found was that the word "their" was incorrectly spelled. This poorly reflects the professionalism that our company desires."

5. Pause and ask for his thoughts on what you said and what he can do to fix it.

6. Suggest action steps. For example, "Next time, I would recommend having someone else on the team review the work before you submit it to the client, or use the spellcheck function."

7. Pause and ask for his thoughts about the action steps. Make sure you both agree on how you will proceed. Document the action steps in an e-mail so you are both on the same page.

 Be respectful by never providing feedback in a group setting.

How to handle social events with men

Men are always attending social or sporting events together. If you don't stick your neck out and go with them, you will get left out of this important relationship building time. Meet the families of the people you work with and get to know the men on your team on a more personal level instead of just small talk in the office. There is something really important and special about eating together where people can relax and become more comfortable around each other. But, there is a tendency for women to hang out only with the other women they work with because that's who they are more comfortable with. As a female manager, it is important that you develop working relationships in and outside the office with both the women *and* men on your team.

Why attending social events is important

Sara Laschever, co-author of *Women Don't Ask* says:

> "One of the biggest things that holds women back is the lack of access to the networks that men have. Women are typically excluded from the social and professional networks in which men exchange a lot of information including advice and guidance."

Networking isn't about schmoozing and being sleazy. Networking is about building relationships before you need them. If you do a good job building relationships with the men on your team, they will be happier to go out of the way for you at work because they trust you and consider you a "friend." Social events are a great opportunity to ask questions and really get to know the men who work for you outside of the office.

If you think you are too busy or already see the men on your team enough in the office, think again. Go to the social events that the men go to. You will be surprised at the conversations that might come up and what you learn when the men who work for you become a little more relaxed after a couple of drinks.

 Think about the people that you want to get to know better before the event. Make time to get to know the males on your team who may usually be introverted at the office. Social events are usually a place where you might be able to get to know them better since it is a more relaxed and comfortable environment.

Etiquette for attending office parties with men

Office parties can be a lot of fun or horribly awkward and stressful. You can ruin your reputation with one wrong move, which is why you want to be on your best behavior around the men who work for you. Once you are a manager, you need to begin to think of these office parties as an extension of work.

Office party Dos	Office party Don'ts
Do use the party as an opportunity to really get to know the men who work for you.	Don't talk about work.
Do have a good time!	Don't drink too much (two drinks max).
Do remember that you are the boss and the men who work for you will be particularly aware of your actions.	Don't flirt with the men you work with.
Do act and dress with class.	Don't wear a short skirt or show cleavage. Always wear a professional dress even if it isn't the office. You want the men you manage to see you as professional (not sexy).
Do feel free to leave early. Just because you are the boss doesn't mean you have to stay until the very end.	Don't gossip about anyone else. Don't get stuck only talking to the men's wives just because you feel more comfortable talking with women.

Most people in the office are so stressed during the work day that they forget to make the time to get to know each other. All of my work relationships improved dramatically after social events. Even though the introvert in me really did *not* want to go, I knew it would be good to get to know the people who worked for me on a more personal level. My office relationships improved straight away because I got to know them so much better. It established trust between us and, ultimately, helped get things done more efficiently.

Remember to volunteer information about yourself so that people can get to know you better as well. Try to make your employees comfortable around you because they may be nervous and quiet around the boss. If you are relaxed and enjoying yourself, they will begin to enjoy themselves as well.

What to do when...

Here are some questions and answers to other common management situations:

> Question: What should I do when a male employee offers me a drink?
>
> Answer: This isn't a date and you don't want it to appear like a date. In order to *not* show favoritism to any employees on your team, you should try not to accept a drink from anyone that works for you, male or female.

> Question: What should I do when a male employee is drinking too much and acting inappropriately?
>
> Answer: Tell the employee that he should head home and ensure he has appropriate transportation. If you still feel uncomfortable with the situation, set up a meeting with him at work the next week. Approach the conversation professionally and without judgment. Detail the events that happened and give him some time to think about it. If he has expressed regret and promises that it won't happen again, try not to let it affect your management of him in the office.

> Question: What should you do if a male employee makes an unwanted sexual advance?
>
> Answer: The most important thing you can do is to catch this immediately before it turns into sexual harassment. Try to resolve this situation right away with a conversation. If you feel comfortable enough, you can use humor to try to keep the working relationship on a positive level and say something like, "Were you flirting with me? I hope not, I really like working with you." If humor is not working, be very clear and straightforward. Tell him that you are not interested and your relationship needs to stay professional. If he continues to hit on you, contact Human Resources.

> Question: How should I conduct a performance review with a man?
>
> Answer: A performance review with a man should not be very different than a performance review with a woman. The only thing that might become different is how the man will react to feedback. Make sure that you are direct and that you don't sugarcoat negative feedback. Have concrete evidence to back up what you are saying and stay confident in yourself. Never show doubt if he gets defensive.

> Question: How should I handle rude jokes and comments?
>
> Answer: Never laugh at the joke if it is rude. Stay calm and tell him that you think the joke is inappropriate for work. If he persists telling the rude jokes that you are uncomfortable with, tell Human Resources.

➤ Question: How should I handle team meetings with men?

Answer: Short and sweet. Keep the small talk to a minimum. Make sure that you get straight to the point quickly and if the meeting ends early, that's OK.

Negotiating with men

Being the boss means that the men on your team will most likely be asking you for something or the other. Men are more likely to negotiate than women to get what they want, so there will be a lot of opportunities for you to use your negotiating skills.

First, *never* be scared to negotiate. Many women are afraid of negotiating and avoid it at all costs. But men respect women more if they negotiate with them instead of just stepping back and giving them what they want without a fight. Don't be a pushover!

According to Sara Laschever, co-author of *Women Don't Ask*:

"The best tactic for women who feel nervous or uncomfortable about negotiating is to practice. Practice moving away from what you are worried about and into joint problem solving. Joint problem solving is when both parties are truly happy with the end result of the negotiation. That is really the best type of negotiation. If you practice, not only do you plan and rehearse things to move to the direction that you want it to go, but if in fact some of those things that you are afraid of happening in the negotiation do end up happening, then you won't be surprised."

Differences in negotiating between genders

Women are more relational and collaborative in negotiations. Women will use small talk at the beginning of a negotiation to develop a relationship before they get down to business. Men, on the other hand, will get right down to business. Men want you to get to the point as quickly as possible and the small talk really doesn't accomplish that. Men can also be more competitive than women so they may be more focused on winning than a woman is.

According to Lee E. Miller and Jessie Miller in their book, *A Woman's Guide to Successful Negotiating*:

"Negotiating turn-ons for men are getting right down to business, letting him go first, finding out what he is interested in and showing that you can get the deal done. Negotiating turn-offs for men are whining, crying, engaging in too much small talk, challenging him head on or threatening him."

Here is a chart that shows the differences in negotiating styles between men and women. (Note: these are the typical trends observed between genders, but it is not always the case):

Men	Women
See negotiating as a game or a challenge	See negotiating as an unpleasant chore that they want to avoid at all costs
See negotiating as an opportunity to show off their skills to their boss	Worry more about protecting relationships
Believe it is up to them to make sure they get what they want	Wait for someone else to give them what they want rather than ask for it
Confident when faced with rejection or criticism	Confidence fluctuates more with criticism and are more afraid of being turned down
Care less about the relationship and think more of the negotiation as a business deal or a sport	Want to work out a solution that is best for all involved
Will make the negotiation shorter rather than longer	Will take more time in a negotiation to make it right

Now that you know the differences between how men and women negotiate, you can now learn how to negotiate with the men you manage.

Top tips for successful negotiation

Many men do not want to lose to a woman, which makes negotiating with men even more difficult.

Here are some ways to successfully negotiate with a man:

> Know all the factors involved before making a decision. Think about his behavior and communication style from previous meetings and negotiations. Try to brainstorm his negotiation style and what he will want beforehand.

> Don't worry about trying to please everyone. Be thorough, but also remember to be decisive and don't circle around the most important topic.

> Establish credibility first. At the beginning of the conversation, show that you have knowledge in the subject area. For example, if it is a salary negotiation, tell your male employee that you are aware of his achievements over the last year and list them.

> In some cases, you may not be able to come to a mutual agreement that all are happy with. Some men just won't budge and you won't be able to convince them of your argument. Try to turn it into a win for both of you, if possible, in another way. Suggest something else that he might be happy with. Try to make a favorable agreement for all involved.

> Try to reach an agreement as quickly as possible with a male employee.

Make men feel comfortable. Gail Evans, author of *Play Like a Man, Win Like a Woman*, says: *"Give them the first question or request, which is usually a minor point. This allows him to relax and think it will be easy so he might drop his guard. He then feels he has to give you something in return.   It is better to fight him on the fifth point rather than the first."*

Self-evaluation

Now it's time for some self-evaluation. By answering the following questions you'll reaffirm your knowledge of how to successfully handle common management situations:

1. How can I provide feedback more effectively to the men I manage?
2. How can I get to know the men I manage better?
3. Are there social events going on around the office that I need to attend?
4. Do I need to create social events to help me connect with the men on my team?
5. What are some negotiation strategies I can use the next time I negotiate with my male employees?

Summary

In this chapter, you learned:

➤ How to provide feedback to men

➤ How to handle social events with the men on your team

➤ How to negotiate with men

> *"Show class, have pride and display character. If you do, winning takes care of itself."*
>
> —Paul Bryant

Conclusion

Today, I really look forward to going to work with my all-male team. Just last week I laughed so hard as the guys made some funny practical jokes on each other. A few years ago, I never would have been let in on the inside jokes nor would I have let myself relax enough to laugh and enjoy myself at work. I have realized that it is ok to join their "boys' club" but still maintain my femininity and professionalism. I have also gained trust and respect, so I hear of more opportunities that are available and I am continually building my reputation.

Congratulations on completing this book and taking your management career into your own hands. Your time is now and I can't wait to hear about your future success as a powerful and influential female leader. As you proactively take the steps mentioned in this book, more and more leadership opportunities will be available for you. And the best part is, you won't have to strain as hard to get them because you will successfully be using your strengths, you will be more confident in yourself, you won't make the common mistakes other women make and, most importantly, you will help the men on your team thrive and be successful, making you a great success as well!

> Index

Made in the USA
San Bernardino, CA
29 October 2014